GREAT SEX

How to Maintain Sex and
Intimacy in Marriage

By
Dr. Gail Crowder

Great Sex

How to Maintain Sex and Intimacy in Marriage

Copyright 2022© by Gail Crowder-Gail Crowder LLC. All rights reserved. No part of this book may be reproduced, photocopied, stored in a retrieval system or transmitted in any form by any means without the prior written permission of the publisher.

Book Cover Design, Interior Layout, and Editor – Latrincy Bates

Published by G.A.I.L Publishing LLC
www.gailcrowder.com

Publishing Logo design by Marie Mickle

Disclaimer:

Certain suggestions are made in this book. While these are intended to be helpful to the reader, the reader must assume all risk associated with following any particular suggestion. Therefore, in purchasing this book, the reader agrees that the authors and publisher are not liable or responsible for any injury or damage caused by the use of any information contained herein. This book is not intended as a substitute for the medical advice of physicians. The reader should regularly consult a physician in matters relating to his/her health and particularly with respect to any symptoms that may require diagnosis or medical attention.

Printed in the United States of America

ACKNOWLEDGEMENTS

I would like to thank my Lord and Savior, Jesus Christ, for giving me this creative mind, and for allowing me to walk out this predestined journey to help wives and couples bring Intimacy and AMAZING SEXY back into marriages all over the world. To my husband Gil, my best friend, my lover, and my sounding board; I thank you for being the man of God that you were called to be, and for allowing me to be just me. To my two sons, Justin and Joshua; Mommy loves you more than life. To my mother, Sharron J. White (R.I.P 2017).;thank you so much for believing in me when I didn't believe in myself, and for helping to finance these dreams that live inside me. I am forever grateful. To my Dad Larry P. White thanks so much for allowing me to talk for hours on the phone with you about my dreams for my business. To my Aunt Clarice B. Jackson; thanks for teaching me your grace and elegance. You are truly timeless. To my brothers Jeffery and Roger (R.I.P. 2016) It was NOT easy growing up between two boys and being the only girl! But I thank you both for teaching me to be strong and to fight for what I want out of life! I love you both!

To my sisters not by birth but by spirit – Sonya, Latrincy, Evette, Joy, Val, Kim, Judy, DeJuan, Chris, Kiki, Lisa. Tawawn and Shawn -- thank you for being a pain in my you-know-what! (Smile) For your prayers, your laughs, your tears, your ideas, your phone calls, your support, your helping hands and your love, I am truly grateful. Thank you, thank you!

To Latrincy Bates the best virtual assistant a small business could ever have. Thanks so much for your skills! You make my life so much easier and my business run smoother!

To all my One Sexy Wives who purchased this book; I pray that this book will enhance and enrich intimacy in your marriage and your sex life to take it to the next level.

With love,

Hail

CONTENTS

1. ACKNOWLEDGEMENTS 4

2. COMMON COMPLAINTS ABOUT SEX 9
   - SEXUALLY INTIMACY HAS BENEFITS 10

3. THE PHYSICAL ASPECT 12
   - SELF CONFIDENCE 13
   - DIET AND EXERCISE 15
   - PAMPERING YOURSELF 19
   - ENERGY LEVELS AND GREAT SEX 21
   - OPTIONS FOR ENHANCING SEXUAL EXPERIENCES 23
     - PRESCRIPTION MEDICATIONS 25
     - *NATURAL OPTIONS* 26
   - FOODS THAT ENHANCE SEX 28

4. THE EMOTIONAL ASPECT 29
   - KEEPING THE CONNECTION STRONG 31
   - THINKING AHEAD 34
   - SENDING THOSE SIGNALS 36
   - DATING YOUR SPOUSE – BUILDING ANTICIPATION 37
     - *SCHEDULING* 37
   - FLIRTING – HIGH AND LOW TECH 40

5. SETTING THE ATMOSPHERE 42
   - ROMANTIC TIPS AND IDEAS 43
   - AROMATHERAPY AND SCENTS 44
   - LIGHTS 47
   - BEDDING 48

MUSIC AND LOCATION	49
MUSIC	49
LOCATION	49
FOREPLAY STARTS EARLY WITH TOUCH	50
MASSAGES TO SET THE MOOD	53
ROMANTIC OVERNIGHT GET-AWAYS	55
SEXY LINGERIE FOR MEN AND WOMEN	55

6. **LEARNING ABOUT EACH OTHER** 57
    - EXAMINE FANTASY OPTIONS AND SEXUAL WANTS 58
    - TALKING BETWEEN COUPLES 60
    - NEW IDEAS FOR THE BEDROOM 62
        - COMFORT LEVELS AND ZONES 62
        - FITNESS LEVEL 63
        - PACE YOURSELF 63
        - DON'T FEEL PRESSURED 63
    - ROLE REVERSALS 64

7. **PRACTICAL CONSIDERATIONS** 65
    - TAKING STOCK OF CHANGES AND CELEBRATING 67

8. **ABOUT THE AUTHOR** 69

Maintaining an intimate relationship with your spouse is an important part of keeping your marriage vibrant and exciting. However, no matter what your intentions may be, there are times in the relationship where your sex life may not be where you want it to be. While some couple's may decide that this is a serious problem or even a relationship breaker, the vast majority of couples invest in each other and work to improve their sexual relationship.

COMMON COMPLAINTS ABOUT SEX

The most common complaints from couples about their sex lives include:

- The relationship is boring He/She isn't interested in sex anymore
- We have sex – on special occasions
- Having a family is just too tiring to have a good sex life
- Couples our age don't have sex
- I want to try spicing things up but he/she has said no in the past
- I don't feel good about my body anymore
- Low libido or lack of sex drive due to physical or emotional issues
- Stress, fear and anxiety about life in general
- Conflicts within the marriage outside of the bedroom
- Medications that decrease libido and performance

Many of the issues mentioned above are perfectly normal and a part of a long term relationship. People do become familiar with each other, fall into a comfortable pattern of intimate relationships or even slowly move away from sexual intimacy.

"I fell in love with the way you touched me without using your hands." ~ Unknown

SEXUALLY INTIMACY HAS BENEFITS

Research has shown that couples with an active sex life tend to live long, have stronger emotional connections to each other, have a lower divorce rate and remain healthier even as they age. So, despite what may seem a natural progression to a relationship, there is sound evidence that keeping a healthy, active and satisfying sexual relationship with your spouse is really a benefit all through your life. It is important for couples to realize that every individual is different and rarely are two people completely matched with regards to their sex drive. Learning to read your spouses signals as well as giving out the right signals yourself is a true skill and one that can help form a much better relationship.

Taking care of your physical self as well as your emotional self is a major factor in being active and involved in an intimate relationship. Some of the work needs to start with you before you can expect to see a change in your spouses responsiveness. However, if you both begin to consciously change your attitudes towards your intimate relationship you will be amazed at how you can discover each other all over again. One key issue for couples to keep in mind as they work to improve their sex life is that they shouldn't be trying to compare themselves to statistics and information that they may find on the internet or in books. Everyone is different and there is no reason that you have to match the national average for number of times a couple has sex. Interestingly enough in a recent

Women's Day report in February of 2010 people report that the average number of times they had sex per year was one hundred and three, which is roughly once every 3.5 days. In addition researchers have found that the more often people have sex, the more likely they are to want more sex. Withholding sex from a partner, either willfully or because of physical or emotional issues, will result in a decrease in the likelihood of sex. Increasing your attention to your partner and sending a clear message that you are in the mood will simply enhance the chance of more frequent intimate moments.

This book will provide simple, effective and yes, even practical, ways to jump start your sex life again. You can start out slowly and stay within your comfort zone at first, but remember that the more you try the more likely you are to create that wonderful experience for you both.

THE PHYSICAL ASPECT

All married couples have some type of Intimate and physical aspect; however this is the area where most couples report having difficulty as their relationship continues over time. There are many different factors that influence the physical aspect of a relationship. While not all physical issues could or should be modified, there are lots of ways to enhance your own personal physical confidence as well as that of your spouse. This chapter will look at some of the significant ways in which men and women can work towards creating a better physical relationship. Not surprisingly many of these techniques and ideas focus on health and healthy living, but also on emotional and mental health issues as well.

SELF CONFIDENCE

When an individual doesn't feel good about themselves it is hard to enjoy a physical relationship. Often self confidence, also known as self esteem or self-worth is a very complex emotional component in an individual's life.

People that have a high level of self confidence are more inclined to:

- Try new things
- Speak their mind openly about their sexual desires
- Respond to their spouses needs and desires
- Get into a romantic mood
- Be spontaneous
- Focus in on their spouse
- Enjoy sex
- Have a healthy and positive view of their own body and their spouses body
- Learn about enhancing sexual experiences
- Engage in foreplay

Both men and women with good levels of self confidence are also more likely to use physical touch and eye contact with each other throughout the day to send those signals that the evening is sure to be special. Self confidence and self-esteem aren't something that you can just snap your fingers and add to your repertoire. However, you can start by avoiding comparisons of your body and physical attributes with others. Often the biggest cause of loss of self confidence, particularly with women, is comparing ourselves to models, actresses and other women. While most people understand in their hearts that looking like a twenty something model is unrealistic, somehow the message isn't getting to the brain. Instead, listen to your spouse and respond to those positive comments about your looks and your body and just stop comparing yourself to anyone else. Couples that find each other attractive both mentally as well as physically are much more likely to engage in frequent sex, so having a positive sense of who you are will really help.

DIET AND EXERCISE

Staying in good shape is always going to boost both your self confidence mentally and your willingness to have physical contact with your spouse. In some marriages lack of physical contact is really noticeable if one spouse feels "fat", "unattractive" or "undesirable" because of their weight. Dieting isn't recommended, especially the crash diets that promise huge weight loss amounts in very short periods of time. Rather, consider a lifestyle change that involves becoming more active as a couple and also making healthier food choices. By working on improving your healthy lifestyle you will not only see changes in your physical body but you may also discover new ways to build in time together. Couples that do more activities together tend to have stronger emotional and physical relationships, so it actually will address more than one aspect of your intimate life at the same time.

Diets that consist of a balance of fresh fruits, vegetables, lean meats and proteins and whole grains can also help the body function more effectively. Minimizing refined sugars and carbohydrates as well as limiting the intake of stimulants such as caffeine will also help with keeping your body in balance. While a glass of wine or a social drink isn't going to be a problem, overconsumption of alcohol will cause a decrease in your overall sex drive and will also impact on other aspects of your relationship as well.

Keep in mind that developing a healthy lifestyle and increasing your activity level doesn't mean you have to go into training or just jog every day. There are many great fun and relationship building activities that couples can do together to get in shape and build those emotional bonds.

Suggestions for fun, moderate to high exercise level activities you can do together

- Going for a romantic walk at the beach, lake, park or even around your neighborhood
- Camping and hiking together through the mountains
- Kayaking or whitewater rafting
- Cycling Going swimming
- Horseback riding
- Roller skating or ice skating to your favorite music dancing
- Taking out a gym membership together
- Playing your favorite sports on a co-ed team
- Water Skiing or snow skiing get-aways
- Gardening and working together on the yard , jogging or running in a charity event as a team Yoga classes

Exercising together in playful yet active types of events is a great way to bond emotionally while you are gaining a better body and a healthier lifestyle. Don't forget that being in better physical shape translates into benefits in the bedroom.

Research has shown that exercise has a positive impact on:

1. **Stress reduction**

    Less stress means more time to focus on your spouse and enjoying the time you are together. Stress also decreases sex drive, so eliminated stress from you life is essential to building a better physical and emotional relationship.

2. **Endurance**

    When you exercise on a routine basis your muscles build up greater endurance to physical movement and activity. This means that you will be able to stay in one position for longer or even be more adventurous in the positions you try out for the first time.

3. **Cardio**

    When your heart is strong and actively pumping blood you have more energy and are less easily fatigued. This will also increase your body flow to all the parts of your body, enhancing the physical and sexual experience.

4. **Strength**

    Like muscular endurance, being strong enough to support your body in a variety of different sex positions is one of the best ways to feel confident and comfortable in trying out new positions.

5. **Hormones**

    Men and women that routinely work out tend to produce more of the endorphins or pleasure hormones. These hormones contribute to the enjoyment of sex and also to getting into the mood.

Interestingly enough, sex itself is a good form of exercise. It is estimated that fairly vigorous sexual activity will burn approximately two hundred calories per thirty minutes. While this isn't the same as a half hour on the treadmill, it will continue to improve your cardio, strength, endurance and calorie burning capacity.

PAMPERING YOURSELF

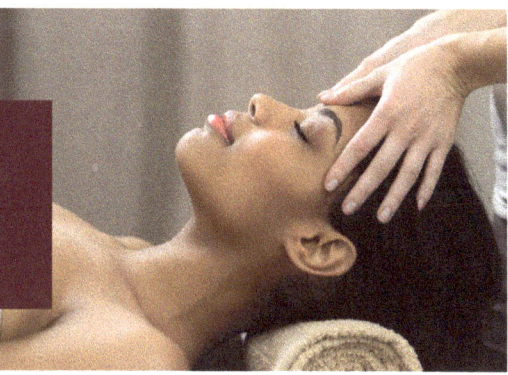

Part of the physical aspect of sex is to feel good about yourself. While most people continually work on their weight and body shape, you still need to pamper yourself physically to really enjoy sex. Pampering yourself starts with making yourself feel sexy. For women this can include taking a long, luxurious scented bath. Often this includes candles, a glass of wine and perhaps some romantic music.

You may also want to consider a pedicure and manicure, a trip to the spa once or twice a month and perhaps a facial on a routine basis. Men should also take the time to feel great about themselves to help get in the mood. Include a massage, a facial and shave, perhaps a manicure or a trip to the spa.

Both men and women can also try a range of different fragrances that often have very interesting effects on both their own mood as well as that of their spouse. Since the sense of smell is one of the most primitive senses, it can evoke strong mental images, moods and desires. Finding a fragrance that stimulates your spouse can really help to set the mood and allow you to also feel great. Taking care of your body is a way to show your spouse how much you care about them. Try some additional little tricks such as smoothing your elbows, knees, hands and feet to provide additional softness during intimacy and foreplay.

There are a wide variety of products on the market today that can really help all skin types feel smooth and luxurious with or without adding a fragrance. If you are wearing a favorite perfume or cologne opt for a non-scented skin cream or lotion to avoid having too many different scents at one time. You may also want to consider having a couple's day at the spa as a way to pamper you both at the same time.

Engage in some relaxing massages, facials and even a relaxing time in a sauna or one of the heated baths at the spa. You don't need to do everything together, do something just for yourself and plan to make it a day of luxury and spending relaxing time together with the anticipation of a wonderful evening together when your spa day is done.

ENERGY LEVELS AND GREAT SEX

As mentioned in the exercise information before, having a high energy level means longer, more satisfying sexual interactions. However, high energy levels doesn't mean having sex in a rush. High energy levels do, however, allow you to enjoy vigorous, extended sexual intimacy that is the key to satisfaction for both men and women.

One of the best ways to ensure that you have high energy levels is to get enough rest. Enough rest is approximately eight solid hours of sleep per day every day of the week. If you have kids, are a light sleeper or have health issues that make sleeping for eight hours difficult, you may simply have low energy levels which decrease libido and enjoyment in sex. Try to change your schedule and talk to your doctor about how you can safely and naturally get the recommended sleep level per day. In some cases herbal teas, yoga, relation techniques or just adding a bit more exercise to your day can really help out in getting a better sleep.

It is also important to avoid a few things as well. For at least four hours before bed avoid the following:

- Caffeinated drinks such as coffee, tea and most types of soda
- Avoid tobacco or Chocolate – in large amounts

- Sugary drinks including fruit juices from concentrate
- Eating heavy meals
- Stimulate types of medications
- Heavy exercise
- Avoid watching television or playing on the computer for at least an hour before bedtime

Instead, of these types of beverages, foods and activities that can help you get a good night's sleep so you are relaxed, refreshed and energized:

- Drink warm milk or herbal teas
- Take a warm bath
- Listen to soft, relaxing music
- Read a good book
- Eat some fresh fruit or protein at least three hours before bedtime

For some couples sleeping together is not the best way to get a good night's sleep. Snoring, someone that wakes up often or moves constantly in the bed or someone that talks in their sleep can often prevent your spouse from the relaxing night they need. Not only does this lead to tension, stress and even anger but it will decrease energy levels and reduce the chance for intimacy.

Sleeping in different beds or different rooms doesn't mean giving up those intimate interludes. Plan and talk about how your sex life and how it can grow and prosper even if you aren't right next to each other in bed each night. Many couples find that having to think about moving to another room for sex is a great motivator as well as a way to ensure that they do have regular intimacy.

OPTIONS FOR ENHANCING SEXUAL EXPERIENCES

There are a variety of medical and psychological factors that can decrease sexual drive, performance and enjoyment. For many couples this is a never discussed topic but one that certainly should be addressed within the marriage.

It is estimated that approximately 35% of men between the ages of 40 and 70 have moderate to severe problems with impotence, also known as erectile dysfunction or ED.

An additional 15% have mild forms of ED that cause feelings of inadequacy in their sexual relationships. Men also can have a decrease in their libido or sex drive, but this is less common with approximately 15 to 16% of the male population estimated to have a loss in their interest in sex.

Women, on the other hand, tend to have more problems with low sex drive or loss of libido. It is estimated that approximately 30 to 40% of all females over the age of puberty will have some time in their life where they have little or no interest in sex. Often this is hormonal in nature and may coincide with pregnancy, lactation, perimenopause or menopause.

For both men and women stress from work, financial problems, relationships or family can all lead to a period of time where sex just isn't seen as important, desirable or worth the effort. However, research shows that couples that work together to redevelop their sexual relationship and intimacy are more likely to stay together, report being happier and also work through the problem that is causing the lack of desire for intimacy.

PRESCRIPTION MEDICATIONS

Men are actually more fortunate than women when it comes to being able to take a pill to help with erectile dysfunction or other sex related problems. Unless there is a health concern with sex or a possible conflict with other medications men tend to tolerate ED medications very well. Of course there are side-effects to these medications and it is very important for both spouses to understand the signs of a reaction to the medications.

Common medications that are prescribed to help with ED include:
- Viagra
- Cialis
- Levitra

All of the medications work to increase the blood flowing to the penis, allowing for a full, lasting erection. While the medications are different they do work very much the same, typically with good results for men. There are variations in how long the medication is effective as well as how quickly the results from taking the medication will be noted.

Women with low sex drive or loss of libido will soon be able to take their own versions of Viagra. While there are currently no specific prescription medications on the market to deal with the physical side of women's sexual experiences many doctors find low dosage antidepressant medications have a positive impact on female libido.

NATURAL OPTIONS

There are a wide range of herbal, holistic and naturopathic remedies marketed over the internet, in health food stores and even in drug stores. Most of these so called "natural stimulants" or "natural sex enhancers" are not tested in any type of controlled setting so their effectiveness is typically a claim made by the company trying to sell the product.

With that being disclosed, there are some treatments that have been used for many years and in a variety of different cultures around the world. It is essential to talk to your physician before using any herbal supplement as they can have side-effects. It is also important to check there isn't a medical condition that is impacting your sexual pleasure and enjoyment before starting on any of these types of treatments.

SOME OPTIONS FOR NATURAL SEX ENHANCING TREATMENTS INCLUDE:

- Acupuncture – for both men and women
- Arginine – used to increase blood flow and circulation
- Ginseng – more commonly associated with male performance
- Pomegranate juice – high in antioxidants
- Ginkgo biloba – may be suitable for men and women that have low sex drive or libido without sexual functioning problems
- Zinc supplements – may increase testosterone in both men and women
- Vitamin E – essential precursor to the development of the sex hormones in both men and women
- Don quai – for women a traditional treatment for all types of female reproductive disorders
- Yohimbine and Yohimbe – perhaps the oldest treatment for male ED it is potentially dangerous to men that are sensitive to the alkaloid found in the herbal preparation

It is very important to know exactly what is in the supplement before considering ingesting the pill, capsule or even drinking a tea made with herbs. Some of these herbal combinations are very powerful stimulants that may be fatal to individuals with heart conditions, high blood pressure or other metabolic disorders. Avoid any type of herbal supplements until consulting with your doctor.

FOODS THAT ENHANCE SEX

There are some foods that are just romantic and associated with intimacy and desire. Chocolate covered strawberries are probably the first food that comes to mind, but there are foods all over the world that are believed to enhance desire and stimulate sexual activity for both men and women. These so called aphrodisiac foods are found all over the world, some which are actually very common.

Whether or not these foods really can increase sexual desire and get you in the mood is not really the issue. A lot of sexual excitement and anticipation is in the mind, so if eating some of these foods gets you in the mood, why not give them a try?

Foods from different cultures that are believed to enhance sexual desire include:

    Celery Lettuce Arugula Saffron Dark Chocolate Artichokes Oysters Truffles Bananas Strawberries

    Avocado Figs Honey Ginger Raspberries Pineapple Vanilla

In most countries red wine is also considered to be an aphrodisiac, especially when combined with dark chocolate.

THE EMOTIONAL ASPECT

Both men and women report that sex is much more satisfying when there is an emotional connection with their spouse. It is true that this component of sexual intimacy is more important to women than men, but men also want to have a strong emotional bond with their spouse. Forming this emotional connection with another person takes effort, planning and commitment to each other, but the pay off is a very strong emotional connection that translates into a strong desire for each other physically and intimately.

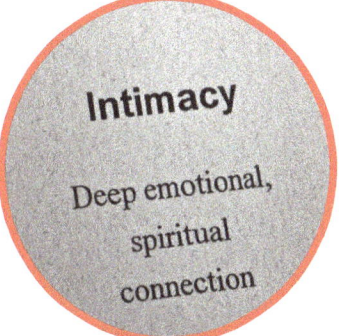

In addition to increasing and sustaining desire, having a strong emotional bond allows more personal freedom within the relationship. Couples are more likely to try new sexual ideas, work harder to please their spouse and strive to keep the physical part of the relationship front and center.

Most couples, especially if they have been married for a significant amount of time, start to forget about all the wonderful things that the other person brings to the experience of being together. You may find you fall into bed at night exhausted from a day at the office or looking after the kids and forget to notice that "come hither" look in your spouses eye. Or perhaps even worse, you notice it but pretend not to since you are tired or really not in the mood yourself.

Over time this gradually leads to both a physical and emotional distance between you. This doesn't mean you can't say no every now and then, but it does mean that you need to find ways to connect emotionally so you will look forward to connecting sexually. It is never too late to start noticing your spouse again, recreating that emotional thrill and excitement you both had when you were together at the beginning of your relationship together.

KEEPING THE CONNECTION STRONG

Emotional connections require work and a conscious effort to reach out towards your spouse on a more than physical level. Keeping an emotional connection strong and alive in your marriage isn't difficult, especially if you develop healthy habits with regards to giving and receiving emotional support and encouragement from your spouse.

Some of the easiest ways to stay connected are to look for ways to highlight and compliment each other throughout the day. A good way to get this started is to make an effort to make one meaningful compliment, notice one positive the other person does, or say thank you to the person for something they did for you each and every day. These words of connection and emotional support and encouragement need to be from the heart, not just hollow compliments to stroke their ego.

Emotional connections require work and a conscious effort to reach out towards your spouse on a more than physical level. Keeping an emotional connection strong and alive in your marriage isn't difficult, especially if you develop healthy habits with regards to giving and receiving emotional support and encouragement from your spouse.

Some of the easiest ways to stay connected are to look for ways to highlight and compliment each other throughout the day. A good way to get this started is to make an effort to make one meaningful compliment, notice one positive the other person does, or say thank you to the person for something they did for you each and every day. These words of connection and emotional support and encouragement need to be from the heart, not just hollow compliments to stroke their ego.

A good communication tool to build a strong emotional connection is to describe the specific behavior, let them know how it benefited you and let them know how much you appreciate their effort. This is much better than just a **"thanks for your help today"** type of statement. It shows not only that you were paying attention but also that you thought enough of the gesture to voice your thanks.

Saying that you love them is also an important part of keeping your connection strong. For some couples saying **"I love you"** is routine, typically when everyone leaves the house for work and when everyone goes to bed at night. Instead of just staying in the routine add an **"I love you"** throughout the day.

Some simple ways to add an "I love you" statement include:

- A note in the briefcase, purse or computer case
- An I love you text message at a random time when the other person is out of the house
- Saying I love you when they get home from work
- Calling them at work or when they are gone just to say how much you love them
- Emails
- Sending a card by traditional mail to their work, just because you care

Keep in mind that for some individuals really public displays of **"I love you"** messages may be more of a turn off than a turn on. Always gauge or watch your spouse's reaction to your communication and make adjustments to keep them in their comfort zone. However, text messages and emails shouldn't be a problem for most people; you may find they secretly look forward to the signal that they have a message or mail.

THINKING AHEAD

If you don't have an active love life, or if it isn't as active as you would like it to be, you may have to start thinking ahead as to how to motivate your spouse. Often spontaneity is great, but for those individuals that work long hours, have to deal with very challenging jobs at home or at work, or those that have a lower sex drive you may have to really plan when the best time for sex.

You may also have to start to think about when the best time for sex actually is for you both. Waiting until after the kids are in bed, dishes done and the work done for the day may leave you both at your lowest emotional and physical energy levels. If this is the case you may want to plan ahead and set the alarm clock a bit earlier in the morning, allowing you to spend time with each other when you are rested, relaxed and rejuvenated from a good night's sleep. You may also want to consider planning for some adult alone time when you get home from work or on those lazy weekends where lounging around in bed and reconnecting with each other is much more possible and less rushed.

Thinking ahead about sex is also a great way to get yourself in the mood. You can find a bit of extra time to pamper yourself that day, getting ready for a special evening enjoying time with your spouse. Remember that a lot of desire and sexual drive is developed through anticipation and expectation, so don't keep your plans a secret. Share your desire for your spouse and express your plans for the afternoon, evening, morning or whenever you want to be intimate. This will only help them get in the mood mentally, ensuring enhanced arousal when it is time to be together.

Thinking ahead if you have children or other's living in your home may be an essential part of being able to relax and enjoy each other sexually. If you have children getting them out of the house may be a priority at least sometimes. Arranging overnight care, babysitters, or for the kids to stay at a friend's house can be a great way to surprise your spouse. This can also be a way for you to really go back to the beginning of your relationship, before parenthood, when you didn't have to be cautious of making too much noise or keeping the bedroom door closed.

While it may sound almost oversimplified, these small little details all send a very specific message to your spouse. They say that you care, you have been waiting for this moment, and you want everything to be perfect for you both. The effort that you make in planning ahead for intimate moments doesn't have to happen every time you make love, but it certainly will be appreciated when it does occur. Thinking ahead also has a lot to do with setting the atmosphere, which is discussed earlier in the book.

SENDING THOSE SIGNALS

While it may sound cliché, most partners can recognize the "come hither" look in each other's eyes. Sending signals early and often that you want to have a romantic interlude is a great way to build anticipation and arousal before the physical contact occurs. Setting the emotional tone for intimacy can start hours or even a day or two before sex actually occurs. Sending signals is perhaps one of the oldest and most instinctual things that humans do, but you can also make them very intentional but yet still subtle, perfect for creating both a bit of mystery and anticipation.

Some signals that will definitely get the message across of your desire for a sexual evening together include:

- Pampering your partner with a favorite meal or food item
- Suggesting a meeting at a favorite lounge or restaurant has a romantic atmosphere
- A long, romantic kiss before going off to work or when getting home
- Dressing sexy
- A visit to their work or office just to say that you can't wait for them to get home
- Extra attention to your physical appearance
- Wearing their favorite outfit or color
- Using messages of love during the day
- Holding hands and touching
- Sharing a shower
- Talking about your desire and your plans
- Long, sexual glances

Giving off as many signals to your plans for intimacy as possible is important. This both cues your spouse as well as helps you to stay intense in your desire.

DATING YOUR SPOUSE – BUILDING ANTICIPATION

For many couples juggling kids, a home, careers and a social life, it is difficult to find time to spend just with each other in the type of romantic activities you could do when you were single or first married. Everything seems to have turned into a literal cycle of work, family, kids and sleep. However, there is a way to bring that anticipation and desire back into your life without having to run away from the kids. Dating your spouse is a great way to set aside planned time with each other. Dates do have some ground rules to ensure they are successful and don't end up sabotaged by kids, family members or your work.

SCHEDULING

Many people don't see scheduling time together as very romantic. Instead they see it as planned, forced or even manipulated. It can also seem to be selfish and perhaps even unfair to kids and other members of the family. However, for your relationship as a couple, it really is an effective way to keep the romance alive in your marriage.

Scheduling dates was normal before you were married, so why shouldn't it be when you are in the same home. After all you don't just show up at a date's home, you call ahead, set a date and time, then everyone can prepare and anticipate the evening, day or afternoon together.

Couples that routinely use date nights wouldn't go back to just trying to squeeze in some romance. Different couples like different options so it is really up to you both to decide what works best. One popular option is to have one night every week as date night. Often this is a Friday or Saturday evening, but depending on work schedules any evening or day is perfect. During this time the couple will go somewhere, and it is important to get out of the house, and spend some quality time together. This often includes going out to eat, dancing, enjoying a drink together or going to a movie, concert, theatre or other type of event.

Some couples prefer to spend time together outdoors. They may choose to go for a hike, picnic, fishing or bird watching. It really doesn't matter what you do, it matters that you enjoy doing it, spend time connecting and get a chance to be alone together.

Other couples prefer to have a more variable schedule. They may take turns alternating between who decides where to go on the date, who contacts who to set up the date and what day of the week it is on. This option typically works best for couples with fairly predictable work schedules that don't have problems in trying to coordinate evenings or days off with each other.

During the date there needs to be some ground rules. During the date the focus is not on the finances, problems with the kids, issues at work or any other types of stressful conversations. This is a chance for the two of you to enjoy each other's company and remember why you love each other so much. In reality it all goes back to keeping a strong emotional aspect to your relationship.

In addition to just not talking about kids, the house or work, you also need to talk to the children and let them know that this is your time alone together. Plan some special events with the entire family as well and your children will understand that date night is for the parents but there will be lots of activities for the whole family. Find a babysitter or family member the kids like spending time with and that you trust, then turn off the cell phones and just go and enjoy. Always have an emergency contact option for the caregiver, but ensure they understand it is only for emergency purposes.

FLIRTING – HIGH AND LOW TECH

Some people are just natural flirts while others have to work at learning the skills needed to be a successful flirt. With all the types of instant communication available to couples today, flirting both high and low tech with relative privacy is very simple.

As mentioned above, flirting by sending signals is really the low tech version of the skill. Those loving, desire filled glances, blowing kisses, dressing in a desirable and sexy way are all low tech ways to flirt with your spouse. Remember that flirting can include conversation, brief physical contact of an intimate nature or by your body language.

There are many ways in which women, in particular, can send suggestive messages just by their body posture and position. For example, touching her hair, face and throat is seen as a flirting type of gesture as it draws the eye towards the location of contact. Giggling and smiling can also be very flirtatious and men are often very clear in sending messages with both their smiles and their tone of voice. New technology has opened up the door for a whole new type of flirting. Texting, chat messages and emails can send a clear message, but it is important to think about where these messages may be viewed and how uncomfortable the message could be if viewed in the wrong arena.

Sending messages that contain obvious or evident sexual connotation in a workplace environment may be a disaster, so always consider the location of your spouse when sending a message.

A good idea is to read through the message as if you hadn't written it and check to make sure it isn't overtly sexual in nature and might be problematic to your spouse if someone saw it. If they could, you may want to reconsider how to word the message so your spouse understands the message but anyone else wouldn't see the flirting component.

SETTING THE ATMOSPHERE

The atmosphere or the environment can be important in sending a message to your spouse or partner that you are in the mood. For some couples a house full of kid's toys, barking dogs or piles of work to do is simply a mood breaker. While you may not be able to totally remove all these obstacles to a romantic interlude you can minimize their impact.

Setting a romantic tone for the evening, doesn't have to be elaborate or stressful. Instead look for ways to make your home more relaxing, seductive and private, a sure way to provide just the atmosphere you need.

ROMANTIC TIPS AND IDEAS

Most people have some tried and true simple ways to make your bedroom look a bit less like a bedroom and more like a romantic spot in the home. Some of the added touches can be great left all the time to help make your bedroom a true sanctuary where you both enjoy spending time with each other.

First and foremost to have a romantic atmosphere get rid of all the technology stuff that isn't romantic at all. The laptop, desktop computer, television, telephone, cell phone or anything else that connects you to the outside world should be temporarily banished. Not only does this prevent interruptions but it also sets a much more relaxing and much less distracting environment. After all you want to be focused on each other and your experience together not on the television or what is on the computer.

You will also want to remove the items in the room that remind you of work that has to be done. The laundry basket needs to be put in the closet or in the laundry room; stacks of paperwork should be put in the office or at least out of sight in a drawer or filing cabinet. This prevents you from letting your mind drift to all the pressures of the outside world that are just waiting for you. Not only will this help with your ability to stay "in the moment" with your spouse but you are also more likely to avoid jumping up out of bed to head back to work immediately after making love.

In addition to removing all those work and daily grind type items from your bedroom there are some additional things that you can add to enhance the enjoyment of the atmosphere for you both. You can try one or all of these things, or even save a few for those very special occasions.

AROMATHERAPY AND SCENTS

One of the strongest of the senses that humans possess is the sense of smell. After all, how many times do you immediately remember a person, a moment or an intense memory when you smell a waft of perfume or cologne, even on a complete stranger? Tapping into the power of your sense of smell can trigger powerful emotional and hormonal responses in both you and your spouse and help to signal that you have a desire to be intimate.

Essential oils used in aromatherapy are a great way to add a subtle scent to the room without being overpowering. Just a small drop or two of the oil on a diffuser or an oil warmer will add a luscious and romantic touch to your next encounter. Some essential oils can also be used in massage oils, however not all oils should be applied to the skin, so be sure to research or talk to an aromatherapist before getting started. Some of the best essential oils recommended to increase the mood and stimulate sex drives include:

Ylang Ylang Used in the East, this wonderfully sweeter smelling oil is popular with both men and women. It needs to be used in very small amounts, one or two drops only, as it can be overpowering for some. Try starting with one drop and increasing if you both find the scent pleasurable. Jasmine Again, a sweeter, flowery smell.

Jasmine is often considered a powerful night flower. While it can be used on its own as an air scent you can also add a drop or two to a warm bath or combine it with sandalwood or a citrus based oil for a wonderful exotic and completely unique combination.

Rose otto This flowery smelling essential oil is one that is great for massage oils, especially for women. It is thought to enhance a woman's libido and strengthen sexual desire.

Lavender Long known for its relaxing qualities, lavender can aid in soothing people that are stressed or anxious so they can enjoy themselves and their time together. Don't use more than a drop or two at a time.

Cinnamon Men in particular respond to the smell of the less floral types of oils. Cinnamon is considered a scent of passion and spice and has some scientific evidence in stimulating blood flow. Other food type scents that have aphrodisiac qualities include vanilla, nutmeg and chocolate.

Cedarwood Another very manly scent, cedarwood is an earthy, sexual scent that both men and women respond well to. You may also want to try sandalwood, which has a more distinctive scent.

Patchouli Very popular with those that enjoy musky yet slightly sweet fragrances. Patchouli is helpful in relieving tension while also stimulating sex drive.

You may also choose to simply go with a favorite perfume or cologne, just be sure not to use too much. In addition avoid mixing multiple scents as the result can be horrific to say the least. If you are using cologne or fragrances on your body dab a bit on your neck, your wrists and your erogenous zones. For most women and men that will be around the breasts, behind the knees and the inner thighs. Again, just a slight amount is all you need as you and your spouses senses will already be heightened.

GREAT SEX

LIGHTS

Romantic lighting is important and should provide a comfortable level of light to allow you to see each other. Love making in the dark is never as satisfying for a couple that wants an emotional connection. Eye contact during foreplay and sex can be intensely arousing, so don't keep you or your spouse in the dark.

Candles have long been a romantic favorite. You can have one or two larger candles or a multitude of smaller candles. Of course there is one concern with candles and that is that they need to be put out for safety reasons prior to you both going to sleep. For some couples a better option is to consider a very soft lighting source such as a bedside lamp with a darker shade that has a dimmer switch. This can allow you to have a soft light that you can turn off easily when you are ready to sleep.

Colors of shades that can help set a romantic mood include the greens, reds and blues, choose one that compliments your bedding and your favorite colors.

Lights that give off a soft glow or a natural light are very soothing and romantic and allow a gentle and almost misty style of lighting. These are often wall mount lights that highlight the area around the bed without making you feel you are in the spotlight. These lights are available in very romantic styles and can even be artificial candle style fixtures that appear to mimic a real flame or old style gas light.

BEDDING

An easy way to add a change to your bedroom is to simply change your bedding. You might want to go for a satin sheet set in your favorite color or a beautiful soft Egyptian cotton sheet set that just makes you feel sexy when you get into bed.

Having a few different types of sheet sets really does have an impact on your love life. After all, if your spouse sees the satin sheets on the bed he or she is already aware of what you have planned for later that evening. This helps to build anticipation and enhances those other signals you have been sending.

Although going out of the house to a hotel, bed and breakfast or even a cabin can be a romantic change of pace it isn't always financially practical or even reasonable. By switching up your bed and making your room look just a bit different you can get that "romantic holiday" feeling right in your own house.

MUSIC

Different couples feel differently about what types of music are romantic. If you don't already have a list of romantic songs you may want to make it a discussion point for your next evening away from the kids or your next car ride together. Creating a list of songs, classical music pieces or even your favorite romantic composers or singers can be a great couple's activity to add to the romance of the bedroom.

LOCATION

While the conversation so far has focused on creating the bedroom as the romantic room in the house, there is no reason why your romantic rooms can't be elsewhere. A lovely evening spent enjoying each other's company by the fireplace or a glass of wine in the den while you relax can all be very romantic locations. Restricting your lovemaking to the bedroom may be, in part, creating boredom and an expectation of routine rather than of enjoyment in being together. Just keep in mind that any room in the home may be the spot for some spontaneous romance, so don't get hung up on just the bedroom.

FOREPLAY STARTS EARLY WITH TOUCH

It is importance to send early, clear messages about your desire as well as building anticipation of your time together are two sure ways to improve your sex life. Another very important aspect of lovemaking for both men and women, but more particularly for women, is foreplay. Foreplay can include flirting as discussed earlier, but it also needs to include some very deliberate types of physical contact. This romantic touch doesn't need to be overtly sexual in nature and for many men and women it really doesn't need to be even subtly sexual.

Human contact is a need that everyone has. This includes both mental and physical contact with others. Sex is the most intimate of that type of physical contact, but also the most satisfying. To increase your sex life start adding a bit more casual touching in your relationship, you will be amazed at the results.

Very socially appropriate types of touching between couples include:

Holding hands This is a very traditional way for couples to remain in close physical contact with each other. Try adding a subtle stroking motion with your thumb or fingers on the other person's hand and see the response that you get.

Hands on the arm or leg A gentle and brief touch on the knee, upper leg or the forearm can be a very romantic gesture. You should also maintain eye contact as much as possible when you make the gesture; this combines both an emotional message as well as the physical contact.

Arms around the waist or shoulders Similar to a hand hold, couples often link arms around their waists or their shoulders to bring their bodies closer together. Try adding a gentle rub on the arm or a slow movement of the hand down the waist or hips to add to the sensuality of the touch.

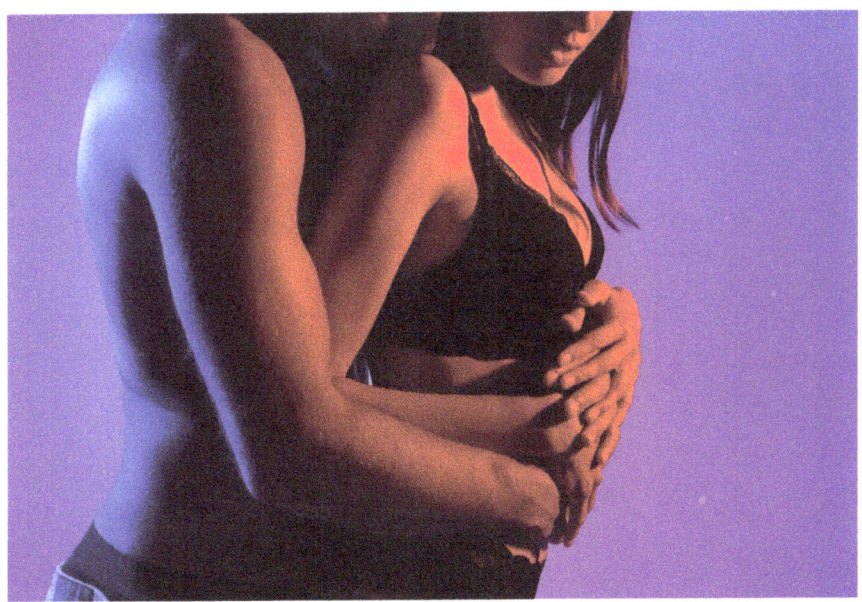

Kissing Kissing, without becoming too extreme, is a socially acceptable way to show your love and desire for your spouse. Just don't get too carried away, especially in work environments as it may actually cause your spouse to be uncomfortable or even resentful of the attention. Talking about what is OK and what isn't and wanting both of your comfort levels are with regards to kissing is an important conversation to have.

Stroking the face or neck Reaching over to run and gentle hand down your spouses cheek or neck is a very sexy move that is also subtle and very appropriate. Again, eye contact will enhance the mood and clearly send an "I want you" signal.

Foreplay in private can be much more sexual and intimate in nature. Full body contact in hugging, kissing and attending to each other is a great way to signal your desire. Of course foreplay can also include undressing each other slowly and sensually as well as giving each other massages or simply exploring each other's bodies.

Foreplay needs to start early and can extend for long periods of time before you actually make love. Many couples admit that sex becomes a routine and an expectation, almost as if it is a timed event rather than an enjoyment of each other. By extending the foreplay outside of the act of intercourse you will extend your sexual arousal and enjoyment, leading to a more satisfying sexual encounter.

MASSAGES TO SET THE MOOD

Massages between couples or even as couples going to a spa or having a massage therapist come into the home are a great idea. Of course if you give each other massages you can incorporate a lot more foreplay and sensual components, which can be a nice added touch.

Massages don't have to be professional quality, rather they simply need to stimulate the other person and signal your desire for intimacy. Massaging the feet, back, legs and arms is a great way to make a lot of physical contact and bring pleasure to the other person. Massages do increase blood stimulation to the muscles being massaged and they are great when combined with a romantic atmosphere to reduce tension and stress and put everyone in the mood.

Try adding massage oils to your massage to add a bit of a change. These massage oils may be scented and infused with the essential oils discussed in the

previous sections or they can be "couple's oils" that heat or cool when applied to the skin. There are also oils on the market that give a tingling sensation to the skin, very sexual and very pleasant for most people to experience. Always test a small area on yourself or your spouse before using the oils on a large part of the skin. In addition avoid using these oils on the genital areas unless specifically indicated on the label for the product.

If you aren't sure how to give a massage or if you have never had a massage yourself you really do need to do some fun research. Book yourself into a spa or have a massage therapist come to the house and experience firsthand just how good they can make you feel. The internet has a lot of great videos and do-it-yourself tutorials on how to give different types of massages. Just go for the basics, after all this is only a part of the foreplay activities, not the plan for the entire night!

ROMANTIC OVERNIGHT GET-AWAYS

If you can afford time away from the house, kids and your busy schedules try a romantic get-away even just for an evening. Plan a dinner at a favorite restaurant, a night at a movie, dancing or just walking along a sunset beach and then plan a night away at a local hotel. You don't have to go far; just a change from the house is all it takes to jump start everyone's love life.

Many people that travel for business have points or rewards programs that entitle them to free nights at hotels. Plan to use these free nights with your spouse, and plan them at different times, perhaps in between stressful holidays or dealing with back to school issues with the kids.

Lots of hotels, even very high end luxury hotels, offer discount rates if you book a night during the week. Monday through Thursday typically will be your best bet for a low cost night at a very extravagant and luxury type of hotel. While you don't have to ask for the honeymoon suite, this could be a wonderful additional romantic touch every now and then. Again, midweek rates and off season rates can be incredibly low cost, often with breakfast or additional perks thrown in as part of the honeymoon suite price.

SEXY LINGERIE FOR MEN AND WOMEN

Sexy lingerie isn't just for women anymore. There are a wide variety of evening wear items for guys as well. Adding a bit of lingerie to your wardrobe collection really does help get in the mood as you will feel sexy and your spouse is sure to appreciate the effort. Finding lingerie that makes you feel sexy yet also comfortable and confident is sometimes a bit daunting. The internet has certainly made this much easier for both men and women since you can buy online and don't have to spend time browsing around through lingerie or costume stores. Keep in mind that some lingerie is often found in costume outlets for a fraction of the price.

Lingerie for women can include those revealing little wisps of lace and satiny fabric, but it can also be lovely nightgowns, teddies and even very traditional types of costume outfits. The sexy French maid, the naughty nurse or the Playboy bunny can all be a great way to surprise your spouse or partner with a night that promises to be anything but boring.

Men have options as well. Lingerie for men tends to stay to the more traditional but thongs, animal print lounging pants and a matching smoking jacket or a really sexy pair of shorts and a form fitting shirt can definitely add to the mood. Satin and silk pajamas for guys are also very sensual and comfortable to wear, great for those evenings around the fireplace.

If you haven't considered adding lingerie for him and her to your evenings together try starting with something basic. You can then decide if you enjoy the experience and add more elaborate types of lingerie and costumes. There are specialty shops that feature leather, vinyl, fabric or custom designed costumes and lingerie styles that are perfect for fantasy evenings. Since you can order online you really can shop the world for the specific lingerie that will help enhance your desire and attraction for each other.

LEARNING ABOUT EACH OTHER

If you have been in your marriage for a while you probably think that you already know all about your spouse. This assumption is what is most problematic in most marriages. You believe you know what they want, need and enjoy so you never bother to ask.

One of the biggest factors in improving your love life and your sex with each other is to actually get to know each other all over again. Forget what you think they like in bed, start exploring as if you were entering into the marriage for the first time. This may seem a little odd at first, however you will soon find out what you want from the relationship with regards to sex as well as what their desires really are.

EXAMINE FANTASY OPTIONS AND SEXUAL WANTS

Talking with your spouse about what they enjoy in sex and what they have always been curious about but haven't tried yet is an important first step. It may be difficult to get the conversation started but with a few tips you will be able to get a clearer picture of what you want and what they want, as well as any fantasy sexual desires you may have.

The following are tips to having a conversation about sex with your spouse:

- Talk about why the conversation is occurring – explaining you want to make your sex life better gives a clear meaning to the conversation.
- Talk about your fantasy sex life as well as ask your spouse for theirs
- Never be judgmental in a negative way or they won't share ideas and their true needs, wants and desires.
- Don't be afraid to ask for more information in a loving and supportive way.
- Give and listen so they will listen and give information to you.

- Start with one thing; you don't have to discuss everything at one time. As you both build up a comfort level with this type of discussion you can become more detailed and specific in the information you share.
- Don't have the discussion in the middle of sex. Have this conversation when you are both relaxed and in a positive mental state. Outside of the bedroom.
- Keep the information private. Don't share your spouses fantasies with your friends or theirs, this is a real trust breaker.
- Incorporate what they want and what you want into each sexual encounter as it makes sense. You don't have to make every sexual encounter into a fantasy night, but you now know how to add that extra spark when the time and mood is right.
- Don't shut your spouse down when they want to talk, especially if this has been something you haven't done in the past.

This can be a bit awkward for you both at first, but with practice and an improvement in your sex life it will become a part of your intimate relationship that just keeps building on.

TALKING BETWEEN COUPLES

Talking before, during and after sex is a part of being connected as a couple. However, not everyone wants talk during sex and not everyone enjoys pillow-talk afterwards.

If you are a talker or if your spouse enjoys communicating during sex you may be able to make that part of improving your love life together. A spouse, or yourself, can instruct the other person how to provide the right amount of pleasure as well as providing highly sexual types of conversation that can help to set the mood. Of course, reading your spouse to see if they are into this type of talking during or after sex is important.

When providing instruction during sex it is important not to come across as bossy, demanding or with an "it's all about my pleasure" type of attitude. Many spouses are very good at helping the other person know what to do in a gentle, loving type of way. In return, they are also willing to follow the other person's instructions.

The taboo about talking or telling the other person what to do to make you feel good is a real problem in many marriages. After all, how would the other person know what makes you feel sexy and is going to result in your feeling of sexual satisfaction if you cannot communicate the information?

If you don't do this occasionally, and it doesn't need to happen every time you make love, you should talk to your spouse about it. You can always make it into a first sex fantasy, playing as if you didn't know anything about the other person and requiring their verbal commands. Reciprocating the communication is part of the fantasy and may lead to much deeper insight into how to improve your sex life and keep each other satisfied.

NEW IDEAS FOR THE BEDROOM

There are a wealth of articles in men's and women's magazines all about how to keep your lover satisfied, new sex techniques and even the top ten ways to turn on a man or a woman. With this kind of readily available information in print and online, finding new ideas for the bedroom isn't difficult for any couple.

Just remember a few basics when planning new ideas, lovemaking techniques or even sexual positions:

Comfort levels and zones

Not everyone is comfortable with a variety of sexual activities. Some people are turned off by different sexual activities that may seem very exciting or even desirable to you. Talking with your spouse and discovering both your comfort level as well as theirs should allow you to make modifications to any sexual activity to keep you both happy and satisfied.

Fitness level

Some of the new ideas for the bedroom may involve a fairly high standard of both fitness and flexibility. If you or your spouse aren't quite there yet this can be a goal you work towards together. Also, just like the comfort level, modifying the sexual position or the technique to match your fitness levels can allow you to enjoy the experience without the pain of pulled muscles, bad backs or aching arms or legs.

Pace yourself

If you are entering into a new part of your improved sexual relationship keep in mind that you don't have to do everything new all at once. There is still time for the old favorite sexual positions and activities, don't forget that they are just as pleasurable as the new and improved techniques you may want to explore.

Don't feel pressured

Lots of couples don't need new techniques or toys, they just need to have more of an emotional and physical connection than they have had in the past. Don't be pressured to stay up with the latest sex position or technique, rather try new things or stay with the tried and true, after all it is your pleasure and satisfaction that counts, not what some editor in a magazine thinks.

ROLE REVERSALS

A great technique for couples to use to spice up their love life without making any changes is to try a role reversal. This doesn't mean that the man assumes the role of the woman or vice versa, but it does mean that the more passive member of the couple becomes the sex instigator while the more sexually aggressive becomes the passive spouse.

This is difficult for both people in the couple since they have to curb their natural behavior when it comes to instigating and responding to sex. The passive spouse, which can be the man or woman, needs to take affirmative action to instigate a sexual encounter. This can really build sexual tension and arousal and will give them more confidence in signaling their sexual desires. The more dominant sexual spouse, again it can be either spouse, will then have to be more passive, a complete switch of roles than can be very stimulating.

Role reversals, like all sexual games and techniques, don't have to happen all the time. They can be incorporated into dates, spontaneous sex or planned sexual encounters between the couple.

PRACTICAL CONSIDERATIONS

As mentioned throughout the book, the more consistently you attend to the sexual relationship you have with your partner the stronger it will become. The more your consider and plan for sex the more often you will have sex and the better it will be for both of you.

It is important to keep in mind that there are many things that can influence an individual's sex drive, and it is essential that as a partner you are sensitive to these possible dips in your love life and don't take it personally.

Many things can negatively impact on sex drive including:

- Medical conditions
- Grief, depression or mental health issues
- Changes in lifestyle (ie. Smoking cessation programs)
- Loss of a job
- Changes in the family structure
- Moving to a new town or city
- Financial pressures

By working together as spouses and not focusing on the sexual component of the marriage you can work together to get back to the love life you both want.

However, once you have worked through those issues you can then refocus on reconnecting sexually and getting your love life back on track. Remember that small steps are the starting point of any change so don't try to take huge leaps, start with those small, small steps.

Date nights are a great way to start boosting your connection with each other. Add more kissing, touching and flirting, even if you aren't planning on having sex that evening. Being more physical throughout the day adds to your anticipation of when you will be together. In addition is shows love, commitment and support, all things that are proven to increase selfconfidence and sex drive.

TAKING STOCK OF CHANGES AND CELEBRATING

While improving your sex list can't always be measured on a calendar or a checklist, you should be able to notice some positive changes that occur. The more techniques, tips and strategies you use to improve your entire marriage the better your sex life will be. Most people mistakenly think that improving your sex life means improving your sexual skills, when in fact the emotional connection as well as your relationship as a couple is just as important.

You typically will notice that you and your spouse are more likely to spend additional time together outside of the bedroom as well. Your increasing physical relationship creates more of a feeling of being a strong couple, working together throughout all aspects of your life.

Celebrating your changing and improving sexual relationship and emotional relationship is only natural. Of course now with all your confidence in trying new things and communicating your fantasies, wants and desires these celebrations are sure to be memorable, pleasurable and every much a reward for all of your hard work.

Take the time to celebrate how close you feel to each other. This can be a terrific reason for a romantic get-away to celebrate your revitalized sex life. Remember you don't have to plan something expensive or elaborate, just the opportunity to get away and enjoy each other will be rewarded .

About The Author

Dr. Gail Crowder is a wife of over 34 years, mother of two boys and, adoptive mother of two girls the Founder and President of Bringing Sexy Back to the Marriage (BSB).

After seeing a need in both secular and religious communities, Gail wanted to create a safe space dedicated to the spiritual and sexual enhancement of marriages for the modern-day wife. Gail has been responsible for spicing up thousands of marriages through the BSB conference and continues to change lives every day.

As an author, Certified Master Sexpert, Marriage and Life Coach, Gail has appeared on dozens of television and radio shows as a specialist and seasoned lifestyle & relationship expert.

Gail has authored several books related to marriage and sex, which include her signature book. "Bringing Sexy Back To The Marriage", and her latest best-selling book, "Keep Your Legs Open: A Wives' Guide to Sexual Satisfaction" and "Praying For The Penis: A Wives' Guide to understanding a Male's Sexual Health". Gail's energy, expertise, and tell-it-like-it is an approach makes her a sought-after keynote speaker and workshop facilitator.

Pick Up Gail's Most Talked About Book on Sexual Satisfaction

KEEP YOUR LEGS OPEN

a Wives' guide
TO SEXUAL SATISFACTION

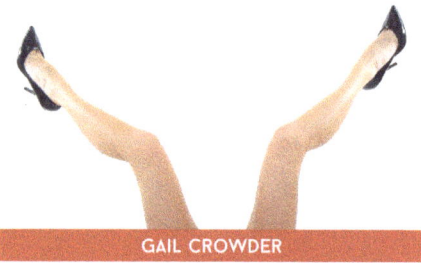

GAIL CROWDER

ISBN-13: 9780983218548

Simple Solutions to Bring Passion, Creativity and Better Sex into Your Marriage

To grab your copy today, visit

BARNES & NOBLE   **amazon books**

For bulk orders of 10 or more copies, please contact us at gailcrowder.com.

Hire Dr. Gail to Speak!
Your Audience Will Thank You!

Signature Topics Include:

From the Boardroom to the Bedroom: Bringing Sexy Back to the Marriage

▼

The Bossy Big Mouth Wife

▼

Should I Stay or Should I Go: That Is The Question?

▼

How to Love Him Without Losing Yourself

Available For:
Keynote Presentation
Breakout Sessions
Seminars & Workshops

For booking information and media kit,
check out the Hire ME To Speak Link on our website at:
gailcrowder.com
Follow Dr. Gail on Facebook, Instagram, TikTok, Twitter, and Youtube.

www.ingramcontent.com/pod-product-compliance
Lightning Source LLC
Chambersburg PA
CBHW040301170426
43193CB00020B/2967